T0031471

marijuana
edibles

Publisher Mike Sanders
Art & Design Director William Thomas
Editorial Director Ann Barton
Editor Christopher Stolle
Cover & Book Designer William Thomas
Photographer Angie Norwood Browne
Food Stylist Nicole Soper
Prepress Technician Ayanna Lacey
Proofreader Georgette Beatty
Indexer Jessica McCurdy Crooks

First American Edition, 2024
Published in the United States by DK Publishing
1745 Broadway, 20th Floor, New York, NY 10019

The authorized representative in the EEA is Dorling Kindersley
Verlag GmbH. Arnulfstr. 124, 80636 Munich, Germany

Copyright © 2024 DK
DK, a Division of Penguin Random House LLC
23 24 25 26 27 10 9 8 7 6 5 4 3 2 1
001-339136-JUN2024

A catalog record for this book
is available from the Library of Congress.
ISBN 978-0-7440-9252-3

DK books are available at special discounts when purchased
in bulk for sales promotions, premiums, fund-raising, or
educational use. For details, contact SpecialSales@dk.com

Printed and bound in China

www.dk.com

MIX
Paper | Supporting
responsible forestry
FSC™ C018179

This book was made with Forest
Stewardship Council™ certified
paper – one small step in DK's
commitment to a sustainable future.
For more information go to
www.dk.com/our-green-pledge

contents

Introduction

Can you believe you're reading a cannabis cookbook?
We can hardly believe we've written one!

What a wonderful world it is that allows us delightful things like marijuana edibles. Despite its clean safety record and numerous health benefits, cannabis is still a bit taboo in many circles. That's certainly changing, and with increased responsible use, we hope minds will continue to open and welcome this enchanting herb.

Cooking with cannabis can be such a gratifying thing. With just a little time and preparation, you can make virtually any dish your heart desires into an edible. However, we love making our edibles as sweets. Not only do they taste just phenomenal, but they are also a great way to end a meal and bring on a wonderfully deep sleep or a fun, wacky game night. You'll be the star of your next "potluck" when you show up with a batch of some delicious, low-dose edibles. (Just be sure to label your goodies so everyone knows they are marijuana edibles!)

We've pulled together some of our very favorite desserts here to get you started in the world of edibles. Whether you're interested in marijuana edibles for recreational or medical reasons, we hope this book helps you find the experience you're looking for.

Acknowledgments

Our thanks goes out to friends, family, clients, and customers who have encouraged our efforts all along the way. We're grateful to Ricard Baca and Aleta Labak for their support and friendship, as well as for bringing Laurie's edible recipes to the world. We'd also like to give a special shout-out to the crews at Oregon's Finest (Megan, Selena, and Andrea—we love you) and GreenSky (Sam, the man!). Alex at ChemHistory is one of our very favorite people, providing reliable testing for all of our cannabis cooking and products. Thank you to our buddy, the talented writer Tyler Hurst, for his no-nonsense advice and wealth of knowledge.

And to you, our open-minded, adventurous reader—we thank you. May this book bring you only good times!

The publisher would like to thank Jeff Soper for his food styling assistance and preparation tips, and Bruce Wolf for his photography of the dispensary shown in this book.

the basics

Marijiuana:
A Crash Course

Marijuana and marijuana edibles are prized not only for recreational use but also for their medicinal benefits.

Plants and Strains

Marijuana is typically categorized by its strains: sativa, indica, and (to a lesser extent) ruderalis. Sativa is known for its energetic, cerebral effects, while indica is known for its sedating, full-body high. Ruderalis strains are low in both THC and CBD, making them worthless for medicinal or recreational use on their own. However, they have an autoflowering feature used by breeders to create hearty autoflowering strains high in THC or CBD. You can also find many hybrids that blend the effects of sativas and indicas into the ideal strain for your mood or requirements. Check out Leafly (leafly.com) or VerdaBase (verdabase.com) for strain information.

Cannabis Sativa

High in THC with long, finger-like leaves, these tall strains are known for their energetic qualities.

Cannabis Indica

These short, stocky strains with wide leaves are known for their sedative qualities.

Cannabis Ruderalis

Ruderalis strains are found in colder regions and contain very small leaves and few branches.

A Brief History of Smoking, Teas, and Ingestion

2700 B.C.E.

A medical book of Chinese Emperor Shen Nung mentions cannabis being used in herbal remedies.

1000 B.C.E.

Bhang, a cannabis drink with the purpose to intoxicate and to enhance sex, is served at Holi, a Hindu festival honoring Lord Shiva.

1100s C.E.

Hashish smoking and eating, featured in *1,001 Nights*, become very popular throughout the Middle East.

Medical Uses of Pot

Cannabis has a wide range of wonderful health benefits. It increases the appetite while reducing nausea, making it beneficial to cancer patients and individuals suffering from HIV/AIDS and cachexia (wasting syndrome). Cannabis also provides pain relief along with anti-inflammatory properties, which is ideal for anyone suffering from chronic pain, migraines, arthritis, PMS, and so on. Marijuana is even valued for its treatment of stress, anxiety, PTSD, and depression. Patients with gastrointestinal issues, as well as those suffering from epilepsy, ALS, and MS, can find relief with cannabis. Studies have also found that cannabis's neuroprotective and neurogenerative properties make it an effective treatment for Alzheimer's, stroke, and Parkinson's disease. While more studies are required to evaluate the level of effectiveness in all of these treatments, the research so far looks promising.

Terminology

Marijuana: Slang for cannabis. It's also known as weed, mary jane, and pot.

Bud: The flower from the cannabis plant. This is where all the medicinal and psychoactive benefits of marijuana come from.

THC: Tetrahydrocannabinol, the primary compound found in cannabis. It's responsible for many of the health benefits, as well as the psychoactive properties.

CBD: Cannabidiol, the secondary compound found in cannabis. It has many amazing health benefits without the psychoactivity of THC.

The bud is the most potent part of the cannabis plant.

1860s C.E.

Cannabis tinctures and hard candies are sold in pharmacies across the United States to treat ailments such as nervousness and to lend inspiration and energy.

1954 C.E.

The *Alice B. Toklas Cookbook* is published, which includes her now-infamous pot brownies recipe. Toklas and her life partner, Gertrude Stein, hosted salons for the Parisian avant-garde.

2014 C.E.

Maureen Dowd of *The New York Times* details her account of eating infused chocolate beyond recommended levels. This serves as a catalyst for tighter restrictions on edibles packaging.

How to Get from
Bud to Brownie

With a few cooking alterations, something that's typically smoked can provide the same high in mouth-watering treats.

How Pot Gets You High

Resin excreted from the cannabis plant contains hundreds of chemical compounds in the form of cannabinoids and terpenes, the most famous of which is the psychoactive cannabinoid THC followed by CBD. They enter the bloodstream and activate receptors throughout the human body, producing the high associated with this wonderful plant.

Effects of Marijuana on the Brain

THC and CBD, the main ingredients in marijuana, attach to receptors throughout the brain and body. Because a high density of these receptors are found across multiple brain regions, you can experience various effects from the drug—for instance, relaxation, increased appetite, poor short-term memory, pain relief, anxiety, and euphoria.

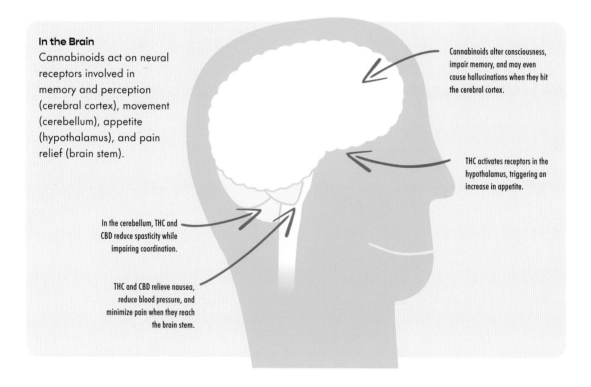

In the Brain
Cannabinoids act on neural receptors involved in memory and perception (cerebral cortex), movement (cerebellum), appetite (hypothalamus), and pain relief (brain stem).

Cannabinoids alter consciousness, impair memory, and may even cause hallucinations when they hit the cerebral cortex.

THC activates receptors in the hypothalamus, triggering an increase in appetite.

In the cerebellum, THC and CBD reduce spasticity while impairing coordination.

THC and CBD relieve nausea, reduce blood pressure, and minimize pain when they reach the brain stem.

The Process

The buds you buy from a dispensary are dried and cured flowers from the cannabis plant. These, as well as shake or trim, can be infused into butter or oil for cooking. But to be effective, the marijuana must first be decarboxylated.

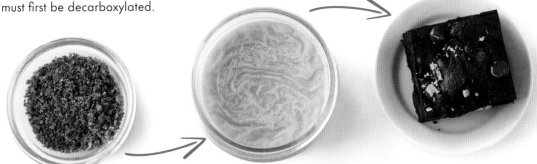

Decarboxylation
To decarboxylate (convert THCA into THC), heat your marijuana in the oven at 240°F (115°C) for 45 minutes.

Infusion
THC easily binds to fats, so it's typically combined with butter or cooking oil. Cook the mixture on low heat for several hours.

Adding Infusion to Recipes
With a few flavor adjustments, you can use canna-butter or oil like normal butter or oil—just be mindful of potency.

Sourcing Pot
If you don't live in a state with legalized recreational marijuana (or in a state with a medical marijuana program, if you're a qualifying patient), finding high-quality cannabis can be tricky. Your best bet is to ask friends who enjoy pot where they buy theirs.

What to Expect
with Edibles

Edibles have come a long way from the old pot brownie, but the basics surrounding their effects remain the same.

Inhaling vs. Ingesting

Whether inhaling or ingesting, the THC must first be decarboxylated (activated from THCA to THC by heat) to be effective. When you smoke marijuana, the burning of the plant matter activates THCA into THC, a psychoactive compound, which is then absorbed into the bloodstream within minutes. This means it affects you more quickly, but it also means the effects diminish quickly. When you eat anything infused with cannabis, however, THC first digests in the stomach and then enters the liver before it's metabolized and absorbed into the bloodstream. So effects take longer to begin after ingestion—anywhere from 30 minutes to 3 hours—but can last several hours.

Smoking leads to a quick but fleeting high.

Ingesting allows you to have a prolonged high.

Edibles Etiquette

 Keep out of reach of children and pets.

 Start with a 2.5mg THC dose of an edible to understand how it will affect you. Wait a day before increasing.

 Too much THC in edible form can stay with you for a while.

 Always label homemade edibles with their potency information.

 Don't send edibles through the mail. It is a felony and puts you, as well as the recipient, at risk of legal action.

 If you bring edibles to a party, tape a sign to the plate indicating what it is (so it won't fly loose) and make sure everyone is aware of its potency.

Effects

Like inhaling, marijuana edibles can lead to a range of effects. While they can differ from person to person and from strain to strain, most people feel relaxation, sedation, euphoria, anxiety, paranoia, verbosity, and increased appetite. It also causes physiological effects, such as rapid heart rate, dry mouth, and/or red eyes. Edibles are thought to cause a higher degree of sedation and relaxation. If too much is consumed, it can result in nausea, dizziness, hallucinations, and severe anxiety.

Not Feeling It?

Everyone experiences effects differently. New users may not feel them as strongly as experienced users—research suggests that ingesting cannabis increases endocannabinoid receptors, which increases subsequent sensitivity. If you find the effects weak, next time increase the butter/oil infusion in the recipe, or use more cannabis in the infusion. A full stomach will delay effects, as will a slower metabolism.

What to Do If You Eat Too Much

Too much THC can be a very unpleasant thing. While not fatal, it can cause dizziness, nausea and vomiting, hallucinations, poor motor skills, and extreme anxiety—not fun. Luckily, the effects will dissipate in time. While you wait for them to go away, try to remain calm and don't drive or operate heavy machinery. Drink water and try to sleep if you can. Otherwise, try to pass the time with pleasant movies or music. For some, coffee and a walk around the neighborhood can help. CBD is known to dampen the effects of THC, so if you have access to CBD oil, it may help you feel more normal.

Terpenes

The complex, flavorful bouquet of cannabis comes from terpenes, secreted in the resin of the plant.

What Are Terpenes?

Terpenes are organic compounds produced by plants. Like cannabinoids, terpenes are excreted in the plant resin and contribute to the overall effect of cannabis. But unlike cannabinoids, terpenes are also found in products people encounter regularly, such as beer (hops) and essential oils. They are what give cannabis strains their unique aromas and flavors, like lemon, mint, pine, and berry. The smell of a strain may tell you about its effects. For instance, pinene smells of, well, pine, and promotes alertness; myrcene, found in mango and thyme, smells earthy and tropical and is very sedating; and limonene is citrusy and a mood elevator. This can give you a way to judge a strain beyond its THC percentage and whether it's indica or sativa.

Savory
Blue Dream
Purple Urkle
Sour Tsunami
ACDC
Afgoo

Spicy
Jack Herer
Trainwreck
Northern Lights
Chemdawg
G-13

Flavor profiles of popular strains
Not sure where to start? Here are a few well-known marijuana strains and how we think they classify in terms of flavor.

Sweet
Girl Scout Cookie
Green Crack
Granddaddy Purple
Pineapple Express
Blueberry

Bitter
Bubba Kush
Harle-Tsu
Shiva Skunk
Agent Orange
AK-47

Sour
Sour Diesel
OG Kush
Headband
Purple Diesel
Amnesia

Pairings

If you understand the flavor of your cannabis, you can know how to best pair it with your food. The best pairing will come if you try a strain including a particular dominant terpene with food containing that same terpene. Eating a mango? Try with a strain high in myrcene. Having a peppery dish? Try a strain with caryophyllene. And of course, citrusy treats call for a strain high in limonene. Really smell your cannabis and let the taste linger. Understanding the aroma and taste of terpenes can make you a true "cannasseur."

Terpenes in Edibles

During the decarboxylation, infusion, and cooking process, most terpenes are lost. While some cooks like to infuse a particular strain to complement the ingredients of a dish, chances are it's not going to make a difference what the original terpenes were. Once it's cooked into a food, it's all about the cannabinoids. The flavors and aromas are subtle enough that you won't notice a difference in the taste of your baked good when using one strain over another. So save yourself time—and possibly money—by keeping to more popular strains. However, if you want to pair a tasty strain with something, try smoking it along with food containing the same naturally occurring terpene.

The Entourage Effect

Terpenes have a wide range of effects, parallel to the prized medicinal uses of cannabis—anti-anxiety, anti-inflammatory, anti-epileptic, pain relief, and so on. Emerging research has discovered that terpenes work with cannabinoids synergistically in the overall medicinal effect of a strain; researchers have termed this the *entourage effect*.

Equipment

With just a few pieces of equipment, you'll be baking edibles in no time.

General Information

For your starting infusions, you'll need cheesecloth, a fine-mesh strainer, and a digital scale. All recipes in this book indicate in the steps any other equipment required to create the dish, so be sure to refer to each recipe for the tools you'll need. While all of these items can be purchased online, you can also find them in your local kitchen and home supply store.

Necessary Equipment

Cheesecloth
This loose-woven cloth is an essential tool for straining your infusions.

Fine-Mesh Strainer
A metal strainer of fine mesh is another invaluable tool for infusing. Look for one that will sit on top of a bowl.

Digital Scale
When measuring your cannabis, digital scales are a necessity. Look for one that will measure in 0.1g increments for expert accuracy.

Parchment Paper
A baker's best friend, parchment paper will prevent sticky situations. It's used in baking as a nonstick, disposable surface.

Other Equipment

Double Boiler

A double boiler is essentially two pans that fit together. The bottom pan is filled with water, while the top pan is filled with ingredients that shouldn't receive direct heat. You can make your own by fitting a heat-safe bowl over a saucepan filled with water—just make sure the bowl doesn't touch the water.

Food Processor

Food processors are powerful and versatile machines—they slice, chop, grind, shred, purée, and mix.

Electric Mixer

Whether it's in the form of a hand mixer or a stand mixer, electric mixers really make your ingredients that much easier to combine.

Candy Thermometer

This cooking thermometer helps you track the high temperatures involved in making candy. It clips to the inside of your pan to monitor the heat for precision cooking.

Wire Rack

Placing a pan of baked goods on a wire rack allows air to circulate under the pan, leading to faster, even cooling.

Microplane

This handheld tool easily removes citrus zest and leaves the bitter pith behind. It can also be used for grating ingredients, such as chocolate.

How to
Decarboxylate

Decarboxylating cannabis is a simple yet crucial step in the infusion process. Heating the plant activates marijuana's psychoactive compound, THC.

1 Heat the oven to 240°F (115°C). (Use an oven thermometer to make sure the temperature is exactly correct.) Roll the buds gently between your palms to crumble them, and place a thin layer of crumbled cannabis on a rimmed baking sheet.

2 Bake for 45 minutes. (After 20 minutes, peer through the top of the door; don't open it fully or heat will escape. Keep checking it every 5 minutes to make sure it's toasting evenly to a golden greenish-brown.) Remove from the oven and allow to cool for at least 20 minutes.

3 Using a food processor or knife, finely chop cannabis. Store in a covered mason jar in a cool, dark place.

Rushed for time?

The slower method outlined above is our favorite method, and should be followed when possible. But in a pinch, you can set your oven to 310°F (154°C) and bake for 15 minutes. This method could reduce the amount of terpenes and burn off valuable cannabinoids, though. Also, you'll want to check more frequently to avoid burning.

Other Methods of Decarboxylation

If you're lucky enough to have a sous-vide machine, you have a way to decarb your cannabis with crazy precision and virtually no cannabis smell. To decarb with your sous-vide machine, place your vacuum-sealed cannabis (grind it before placing it in the bag to be vacuum sealed) in a pot filled with water and heat your sous-vide machine to 200°F (100°C). Once your water has reached the desired temperature, cook for 1 hour before removing your decarbed cannabis.

If you don't have a sous-vide machine, you can decarb your cannabis in the oven using either the method described in the previous steps or the faster version, which involves a higher oven temp.

Doesn't Cooking Within the Recipes Decarboxylate the Pot?

When you're making edibles, decarboxylation is a crucial step. Without it, your recipes are unlikely to achieve their maximum potential potency. While the heat during the infusion and the heat during the cooking in the recipe would activate some THCA to THC, it might not activate it all. So do you need to decarb your cannabis first? We certainly recommend it. However, if maximizing your THC potency is not a requirement for you, decarboxylation is a step you could skip.

How to
Calibrate Infusions

The most critical part of making edibles lies in the calculation of THC per serving.

The Aim of Calibrating

In our kitchen, we cook with 15 percent THC cannabis. The cannabis you cook with in all likelihood is very different—perhaps stronger, perhaps weaker. Either way, if you want a 10mg THC per teaspoon dose (the dose for the edibles in this book), you'll have to make some adjustments. It involves a little math, but it's nothing you can't handle.

How to Calculate the Amount of THC per Serving

Our infusions are calibrated to produce 10mg THC per teaspoon using 15 percent THC. If you have a different percentage, use this table to determine the cannabis-to-butter ratio.

THC (%)	Cannabis (g)
5	21
10	10.5
15	7
20	5.5
25	4.5
30	3.5

Knowing the Potency

Infused butter and oil can be very potent; be careful when ingesting until you know your dosage.

THC Loss During Infusion

During the decarboxylation and infusion process, there is some THC loss. But if you follow our guide, it will be minimal. We've found our butter and oil infusions have a 20 percent loss of THC. So 1g of 15 percent THC cannabis has 150mg THC; however, infused into butter or oil, you'll get about 120mg THC. The biggest key to maintaining potency is to extract at a low temperature.

Cannabinoids and terpenes are excreted in the resin glands of the cannabis plant.

Excessive heat can burn off terpenes and cannabinoids. To maintain potency, keep temperatures low.

What If You Don't Know the THC Percentage of Your Pot?

If you don't know the THC percentage of your cannabis, follow our infusion guides and try a ½ teaspoon to assess its potency. Wait a day before increasing your dose. If you're ready for a 1-teaspoon dose, you're good to go. If you need less, either make a record of that and proceed with recipes using that dosage level, or add more unsalted butter to weaken it. To make the infusion, melt canna-butter and unsalted butter together in a saucepan over low heat, stirring to combine thoroughly. If you need more than 1 teaspoon, make a record of your dosage level and increase the amount of canna-butter in your recipes.

How to Make
Infusions

Butter and coconut oil are the most popular and versatile infusions for baking. The following steps walk you through how to make each type.

Coconut oil is lauded for its health benefits, making it a perfect infusion.

Canna-Coconut Oil

SERVING SIZE 1 teaspoon
DOSAGE PER SERVING 10mg THC
YIELD 12 fl oz (350ml)

Ingredients
14 fl oz (414ml) coconut oil

7g cannabis, decarboxylated and finely chopped

Canna-Butter

SERVING SIZE 1 teaspoon
DOSAGE PER SERVING 10mg THC
YIELD 14 fl oz (350ml)

Ingredients
16oz (454g) unsalted butter

7g cannabis, decarboxylated and finely chopped

1 In a medium saucepan over low heat, heat coconut oil or unsalted butter. Add decarboxylated cannabis and stir to mix.

2 Continue to cook for 3 hours over low heat, stirring mixture every 20 minutes with a spatula.

The oil (or butter) should not simmer, but occasional bubbles are okay.

3 Line a fine-mesh strainer with cheesecloth and place into a deep glass bowl. Carefully pour oil or butter through the cheesecloth.

4 Press gently with a silicone spatula to strain oil or butter from cannabis.

5 Lift the cheesecloth and squeeze any remaining oil or butter into the bowl.

6 Allow oil or butter to cool, pour into a 16-ounce (450g) container, and close with an airtight lid.

Storing Infusions

Canna-coconut oil keeps covered at room temperature for 6 months. Store away from sunlight.

Canna-butter keeps covered in the refrigerator for 3 months or wrapped well in the freezer for up to 6 months. When freezing canna-butter, it's helpful to preportion it into smaller sizes so you can defrost just the amount you need.

How to Cook
with Infusions

With a few simple dos and don'ts, you, too, can master the art of cooking with cannabis in all of your favorite dishes.

In Your Own Favorite Recipes

With a few adjustments, anything can be infused. If you start by making canna-butter or canna-coconut oil as outlined in this book, 1 teaspoon makes 1 serving. Swap as many teaspoons of regular butter or oil for the canna version in the amount equal to the number of servings in the dish.

Adding Infusions
You can swap in infused butter or oil for the regular version. In this case, melted canna-butter is added to batter.

DISGUISING STRONG FLAVORS OF INFUSIONS

Once you've swapped in the appropriate amount of canna-butter or canna-coconut oil, you may need to adjust the flavors to cover the cannabis taste. If your recipe is already a flavorful dish, you may not need to make any adjustments. However, if it's more subtle, you increase the flavorful ingredient(s) or add flavors such as chocolate, coffee, peanut butter, and cinnamon to better hide the taste.

Don't

🍁 Don't bake in the oven above 340°F (170°C).

🍁 Don't microwave on high.

🍁 Don't cook on the stove on high heat or bring infused butter or oil to a boil.

🍁 Don't add too much canna-butter or canna-coconut oil: only 1 teaspoon per serving unless you need a higher dose.

🍁 Don't serve an infused dish without letting everyone know.

🍁 Don't store an infused dish without a sign unless you live by yourself.

Do

🍁 Do swap out 1 teaspoon of butter for canna-butter (or oil for canna-coconut oil) for each serving in the dish.

🍁 Do taste (a very small amount of) the batter to evaluate the flavor.

🍁 Do increase the strongest flavors in the dish to cover the cannabis taste.

🍁 Do increase the cooking time slightly if you've lowered the cooking temperature.

🍁 Do melt the infusion before mixing it into the bowl, whenever applicable; if it's a hard glob of fat, it won't mix properly with other ingredients.

Monkey Mousse

Quick & Easy
Single-Serving Edibles

These single-serving treats are an easy way to create edibles for yourself in just a few minutes.

Monkey Mousse

Combine ¼ cup peanut butter and ¼ cup banana yogurt. Stir in 1 teaspoon canna-coconut oil and top with 1 tablespoon chopped walnuts.

White Chocolate–Dipped Strawberries

Melt 4 ounces (110g) white chocolate slowly in the microwave. Stir in 1 teaspoon canna-butter. Dip 6 strawberries in white chocolate mix and place on parchment paper. Allow to set.

Salted Caramel

Heat 5 packaged caramels (41g) in the microwave until softened and barely melted. Stir in 1 teaspoon canna-butter. Transfer to parchment paper and shape into a rectangle. Sprinkle with sea salt. Allow to harden.

Sweet & Spicy Pecans

Dessert Quesadilla

Fruity Yogurt

Dessert Quesadilla

Spread 2 tablespoons almond butter on two
8-inch (20cm) flour tortillas. Add 1 sliced
banana and 2 teaspoons maple syrup to one of
the tortillas. Top it with the other tortilla. Sauté in
1 teaspoon canna-butter and 1 tablespoon
butter for 5 minutes over medium-low heat,
turning halfway through the cooking time.

Coconut Crunch

Brush an 8-inch (20cm) flour tortilla with
1 teaspoon canna-coconut oil. Sprinkle
tortilla with 2 tablespoons coconut sugar and
2 tablespoons shredded coconut. Bake at 325°F
(170°C) for 10 minutes or until coconut turns
golden.

Fruity Yogurt

Whip 1 cup Greek yogurt with 2 tablespoons
puréed fruit (or jam, jelly, or preserves). Add
sugar or sweetener to taste (optional) and
1 teaspoon softened canna-coconut oil.

Sweet & Spicy Pecans

Sauté ½ cup pecan halves in 1 tablespoon light
brown sugar, 1 tablespoon honey, a pinch of
cayenne pepper, and 1 teaspoon canna-butter
(or canna-coconut oil). Cook for 5 minutes or
until fragrant and beginning to brown. Allow
to cool.

Baked Apple

Core an apple, leaving the bottom ½ inch
(1.25cm) of apple intact. Fill cavity with
1 tablespoon honey and 1 teaspoon canna-
butter. Sprinkle with ¼ teaspoon cinnamon and
bake at 340°F (171°C) for 45 minutes or until
apples are cooked through and tender. It's great
with a scoop of vanilla ice cream!

cookies & bars

Chocolate Malt Cookies

Ingredients

8 tablespoons unsalted butter, at room temperature

8 tablespoons canna-butter, at room temperature

½ cup firmly packed light brown sugar

¼ cup granulated sugar

2 large eggs

1 tablespoon vanilla extract

⅔ cup malted milk powder

2 cups all-purpose flour

1½ teaspoons baking soda

½ teaspoon salt

1 (12oz; 340g) bag semisweet chocolate chips

Dietary Notes

Nut free

Malted milk powder is paired with chocolate chips for these cookies, giving you the flavorful sensation of eating a chocolate malted milkshake.

1 Heat the oven to 340°F (170°C). Line two baking sheets with parchment paper and set aside.

2 In a medium bowl, beat unsalted butter, canna-butter, light brown sugar, and granulated sugar with an electric mixer at medium speed until light and fluffy, about 5 to 7 minutes. Beat in eggs one at a time at low speed until combined. Beat in vanilla extract at medium speed until combined. Set aside.

3 In a large bowl, combine malted milk powder, all-purpose flour, baking soda, and salt. Add to butter and sugar mixture, and mix until just incorporated. Stir in semisweet chocolate chips.

4 Place tablespoon-sized balls of dough 2 inches (5cm) apart. Bake until cookies are set, about 9 to 11 minutes.

For **Malted Chocolate Cherry Cookies,** add 2 teaspoons almond extract and ¼ cup chopped dried cherries to the final batter and bake as directed.

INFUSION TYPE:
Canna-butter
PREP TIME:
10 minutes
COOK TIME:
11 minutes
SERVING SIZE:
1 cookie
YIELD:
24 cookies

STORAGE
Keep in an airtight container at room temperature for up to 5 days.

Coconut & Almond Macaroons

Ingredients

¾ cup granulated sugar

2 large egg whites

2 cups shredded coconut

⅔ cup chopped almonds

5 tablespoons plus
   1 teaspoon canna-
   coconut oil, melted

2 teaspoons vanilla
   extract

½ teaspoon almond
   extract

Pinch salt

Dietary Notes

Gluten free, Passover
   friendly

Coconut and almond flavors enhance this simple treat. Crispy on the outside and chewy on the inside, the texture of these macaroons is perfection.

1 Heat the oven to 340°F (170°C). Line two baking sheets with parchment paper and set aside.

2 In a large bowl, whisk together sugar and egg whites until semi-stiff peaks form. Mixture should have the consistency of marshmallow cream.

3 Add shredded coconut, chopped almonds, canna-coconut oil, vanilla extract, almond extract, and salt, and mix well.

4 Place scoops of mixture 2 inches (5cm) apart on the baking sheets.

5 Bake for 15 to 17 minutes or until golden brown and set.

INFUSION TYPE:
Canna-coconut oil

PREP TIME:
10 minutes

COOK TIME:
17 minutes

SERVING SIZE:
1 cookie

YIELD:
16 cookies

Dip the bottom of and then drizzle the macaroons with melted chocolate for added flair.

STORAGE
Keep in an airtight container in the refrigerator for up to 1 week or in the freezer for up to 3 months.

Amaretto-Dipped Sandwich Cookies

Ingredients

3oz (85g) white chocolate chips

1 teaspoon almond extract

2 tablespoons canna-coconut oil

12 sandwich cookies

Dietary Notes

None

Sweet, salty, crunchy, and creamy, these sandwich cookies have tons of wonderful flavors and textures. The addition of almond extract to the white chocolate makes the coating truly decadent.

1 Line a baking sheet with parchment paper and set aside. In a double boiler over medium heat, stir white chocolate chips for 5 to 10 minutes or until melted.

2 Add almond extract and canna-coconut oil, and stir until thoroughly combined. Remove from heat and pour into a shallow bowl.

3 Working quickly, dip each sandwich cookie completely in melted chocolate and remove with a fork. Let any excess chocolate drip back before setting the cookie on the prepared baking sheet.

4 Allow chocolate to set for at least 1 hour. You can speed up this process by placing the cookies in the refrigerator. Once the cookies have hardened, remove from the baking sheet.

INFUSION TYPE:
Canna-coconut oil

PREP TIME:
1 hour, 10 minutes

COOK TIME:
10 minutes

SERVING SIZE:
2 sandwich cookies

YIELD:
12 sandwich cookies

Add decorative sprinkles, wrap them in cellophane bags, and tie with ribbons to make a great gift.

STORAGE
Keep in an airtight container at room temperature for up to 2 weeks or in the refrigerator for up to 1 month.

Citrus & Almond Florentines

Ingredients

1 medium orange

2¼ cups slivered almonds

¾ cup heavy cream

4 tablespoons canna-butter

¼ cup granulated sugar

¼ cup honey

3 tablespoons orange marmalade

3 tablespoons all-purpose flour

¼ teaspoon salt

½ teaspoon vanilla extract

Dietary Notes

None

TAKE IT HIGHER

These cookies are just begging for a little chocolate. Brush the underside with melted dark chocolate and allow to set on parchment paper for 10 to 15 minutes.

Impress your friends with these easy, crispy lace cookies of bright orange and honey, nutty almond, and caramel crunch.

1 Heat the oven to 340°F (170°C). Line a baking sheet with parchment paper, spray with nonstick cooking spray, and set aside. Wash orange. Using a microplane, remove all zest from the peel, making sure not to get bitter white membrane beneath the orange color. Set aside.

2 Place almonds in a food processor and pulse for 25 to 30 seconds or until a coarse texture forms that's not yet a paste.

3 In a medium saucepan over medium-high heat, stir together heavy cream, canna-butter, sugar, and honey. Stirring frequently, bring mixture to a boil and continue cooking for 5 to 6 minutes or until it begins to thicken.

4 Cook mixture for 1 minute more, stirring constantly, until it begins to brown. Remove from heat. Immediately stir in ground almonds, orange zest, orange marmalade, all-purpose flour, salt, and vanilla extract.

5 Evenly space 6 tablespoon-sized balls of dough on the prepared baking sheet. Flatten balls with a damp spatula or your hand.

6 Bake for 16 to 18 minutes or until cookies achieve a deep brown color. Remove cookies from the oven, transfer from the parchment paper to wire racks, and allow to cool. Line the baking sheet with new parchment paper, spray with nonstick cooking spray, and repeat baking 6 at a time until you've made all 24 cookies.

INFUSION TYPE:
Canna-butter

PREP TIME:
20 minutes

COOK TIME:
1 hour, 15 minutes

SERVING SIZE:
2 florentines

YIELD:
24 florentines

STORAGE
Keep in an airtight container at room temperature for up to 5 days.

Ingredients

2 cups all-purpose flour

½ teaspoon baking powder

½ teaspoon salt, divided

12 tablespoons canna-butter, at room temperature, divided

6 tablespoons unsalted butter, cut into chunks

1 cup firmly packed light brown sugar

1 large egg

3 teaspoons vanilla extract, divided

1½ cups granulated sugar

1 cup heavy cream

2 cups roasted salted cashews

Dietary Notes
None

TAKE IT HIGHER
The bars will be firmer and therefore easier to cut if you place them in the refrigerator for 30 minutes first.

A batter of chewy, rich caramel and salty cashews tops a buttery crust. In a ranking out of 10, these bars are an 11.

1 Heat the oven to 340°F (170°C). Line a 9×13-inch (23×33cm) baking pan with parchment paper and set aside.

2 In a small bowl, combine all-purpose flour, baking powder, and ¼ teaspoon salt. Set aside.

3 In a medium bowl, mix 6 tablespoons canna-butter, unsalted butter, and light brown sugar with an electric mixer at medium speed for 5 minutes or until light and fluffy. Add egg and 1 teaspoon vanilla extract, and beat for 2 minutes at low speed until combined.

4 Add flour mixture and beat at medium speed for 2 to 3 minutes. Press crust mixture into the prepared pan. Chill for 30 minutes.

5 In a medium nonstick pan over medium heat, heat granulated sugar. When you see sugar beginning to color, stir until it's light brown, about 5 to 7 minutes. Carefully add heavy cream and stir until smooth.

6 Turn down the heat to low and add the remaining 6 tablespoons canna-butter, the remaining 2 teaspoons vanilla extract, and the remaining ¼ teaspoon salt. Stir until butter has melted and remove from the heat.

7 Stir cashews into caramel mixture. Pour caramel–cashew mixture into the pan on top of the chilled crust. Bake for 20 minutes or until set. Allow to cool thoroughly before cutting into 36 bars.

INFUSION TYPE:
Canna-butter

PREP TIME:
50 minutes

COOK TIME:
30 minutes

SERVING SIZE:
1 bar

YIELD:
36 bars

STORAGE
Keep in an airtight container at room temperature for up to 1 week or in the freezer for up to 2 months.

Salted Caramel & Cashew Bars

Add a couple tablespoons of chocolate hazelnut spread to the batter for extra richness.

Triple Chocolate & Hazelnut Brownies

Ingredients

1 cup unsweetened cocoa powder

1 cup all-purpose flour

1 teaspoon baking soda

¼ teaspoon salt

2 tablespoons unsalted butter

8 tablespoons canna-butter

1½ cups firmly packed dark brown sugar

4 large eggs

2 teaspoons vanilla extract

½ cup milk chocolate chips

½ cup semisweet chocolate chips

½ cup chopped toasted hazelnuts

Dietary Notes

None

These extraordinarily good brownies are for true chocoholics. Three kinds of chocolate are mixed with toasted hazelnuts to create a super-rich treat with a satisfying crunch.

1 Heat the oven to 340°F (170°C). Lightly coat a 9×13-inch (23×33cm) baking pan with nonstick cooking spray and set aside.

2 In a medium bowl, combine unsweetened cocoa powder, all-purpose flour, baking soda, and salt. Set aside.

3 In a double boiler over low heat, melt together unsalted butter and canna-butter. Once melted, remove from heat and stir in dark brown sugar. Pour butter–sugar mixture into flour mixture and stir to combine.

4 In a large bowl, beat eggs and vanilla extract with an electric mixer at medium speed for 1 minute. Slowly add in butter–flour mixture and mix for 1 minute more or until just combined. Add milk chocolate chips, semisweet chocolate chips, and hazelnuts, and beat for a few seconds to distribute.

5 Transfer mixture to the prepared pan and bake for 23 to 25 minutes or until top looks dark and dry. Cool completely in the pan before cutting into 24 pieces and transferring to a plate.

INFUSION TYPE:
Canna-butter

PREP TIME:
15 minutes

COOK TIME:
30 minutes

SERVING SIZE:
1 brownie

YIELD:
24 brownies

STORAGE
Keep tightly wrapped in plastic wrap in the refrigerator for up to 4 to 5 days or in the freezer for up to 4 to 5 months.

Key Lime Squares

Ingredients

4 tablespoons unsalted butter, at room temperature

4 tablespoons canna-butter, at room temperature

½ cup confectioners' sugar

2 cups plus 5 tablespoons all-purpose flour

1 teaspoon vanilla extract

Pinch salt

4 large eggs, lightly beaten

1¾ cups granulated sugar

¼ cup key lime juice

1 tablespoon lime zest

Dietary Notes

Nut free

Capture Key lime pie taste in these delightfully refreshing bars. The balance of sweet and creamy lime curd with rich shortbread crust makes each bite a sunny experience.

1 Heat the oven to 340°F (170°C). Lightly coat a 9×13-inch (23×33cm) baking pan with nonstick cooking spray and set aside.

2 In a large bowl, beat unsalted butter, canna-butter, and confectioners' sugar with an electric mixer at medium speed for 3 to 4 minutes or until light and fluffy.

3 Add all-purpose flour, vanilla extract, and salt. Mix for 2 to 3 minutes or until well combined.

4 Press dough into the bottom of the prepared pan. Bake for 20 to 23 minutes or until light golden brown. Allow crust to cool for 10 minutes.

5 In a large bowl, whisk together eggs and granulated sugar. Add key lime juice and lime zest, and whisk well.

6 Pour mixture over cooled crust and bake for 23 to 25 minutes or until set. Cool fully before cutting into 12 squares.

INFUSION TYPE
Canna-butter

PREP TIME
25 minutes

COOK TIME
48 minutes

SERVING SIZE
1 square

YIELD
12 squares

STORAGE
Keep tightly wrapped in plastic wrap in the refrigerator for up to 5 days.

For a fun presentation, top with additional confectioners' sugar and lime zest before serving.

Hawaiian Butter Mochi

Ingredients

3 cups sweet rice flour (mochiko)

2¼ cups granulated sugar

2 teaspoons baking powder

¼ teaspoon salt

2 (14oz; 400ml) cans coconut milk

1 cup whole milk

5 large eggs

8 tablespoons canna-butter, melted

2 teaspoons vanilla extract

Dietary Notes

Gluten free

Originating in Japan and extremely popular in Hawaii, mochi is a sweet, glutinous rice cake. The texture of this treat is unlike any dessert you've had before—fabulously chewy and squishy.

1 Heat the oven to 340°F (170°C). Spray a 9×13-inch (23×33cm) baking pan with nonstick cooking spray and set aside.

2 In a medium bowl, combine sweet rice flour, sugar, baking powder, and salt.

3 In a separate medium bowl, whisk together unsweetened coconut milk, whole milk, eggs, canna-butter, and vanilla extract.

4 Add the flour mixture to the egg mixture, whisking to blend. Pour the mixture into the prepared pan.

5 Bake for 1 hour or until lightly golden and brown around the edges. Cool completely before cutting into 24 bars.

INFUSION TYPE:
Canna-butter

PREP TIME:
10 minutes

COOK TIME:
1 hour

SERVING SIZE:
1 square

YIELD:
24 squares

STORAGE
Keep in an airtight container or tightly wrapped in plastic wrap at room temperature for up to 3 days or refrigerate for up to 5 days. Note that the texture might become tougher when mochi is refrigerated.

You can add shredded coconut to the mixture before baking for extra flavor and texture.

pies, tarts & pastries

Orange & Honey Cream Puffs

Ingredients:

1 cup water

8 tablespoons unsalted butter

⅛ teaspoon salt

1 cup all-purpose flour

4 large eggs

2 tablespoons whole milk

1 egg yolk

1½ cups vanilla Greek yogurt

3 tablespoons canna-coconut oil, softened

2 tablespoons honey

½ teaspoon orange extract

1 teaspoon orange zest

Dietary Notes:

Nut free

Greek yogurt replaces the traditional custard filling in these sweet and citrusy cream puffs, giving these delicate treats spectacular flavor.

1 Heat the oven to 400°F (200°C). In a large saucepan over medium-high heat, bring water, unsalted butter, and salt to a boil. Add all-purpose flour and stir for 1 to 2 minutes or until mixture pulls away from the sides and forms into a ball. Remove from heat and let rest for 5 minutes.

2 Add eggs one at a time, beating well after each addition, until shiny and smooth. Using a ¼ cup measure, drop dough 3 inches (7.5cm) apart onto two parchment-lined baking sheets.

3 In a small bowl, beat together whole milk and egg yolk by hand with a whisk or fork. Brush onto puffs. Bake for 30 to 33 minutes or until golden brown. Remove from the oven and allow to cool for 10 to 15 minutes.

4 In a medium bowl, combine Greek yogurt, canna-coconut oil, honey, orange extract, and orange zest. Split puffs horizontally in half with a knife and fill with cream. Replace tops.

INFUSION TYPE:
Canna-coconut oil

PREP TIME:
25 minutes

COOK TIME:
35 minutes

SERVING SIZE:
1 cream puff

YIELD:
9 cream puffs

STORAGE
Keep in an airtight container in the refrigerator for up to 2 days.

For an extra touch of sweetness, sprinkle the cream puffs with confectioners' sugar.

Buttered Rum Apple Turnovers

Ingredients:

2 tablespoons plus 2 teaspoons canna-butter

4 tart apples, peeled, cored, and sliced

1 tablespoon rum

3 tablespoons dried cranberries

4 tablespoons granulated sugar

2 tablespoons all-purpose flour

¼ teaspoon ground cinnamon

Pinch salt

1 (17.3oz; 490g) package frozen puff pastry, thawed according to package directions

2 large eggs

2 tablespoons water

Dietary Notes:
Nut free

Rum gives these flaky turnovers a complexity of flavor you'll just adore. They're best warm with a scoop of vanilla ice cream.

1 Heat the oven to 340°F (170°C). Line two baking sheets with parchment paper and set aside.

2 In a large sauté pan over medium-low heat, melt canna-butter. Add tart apple slices and rum, and sauté for 5 minutes. Stir in dried cranberries and sugar, and cook for 3 minutes more. Transfer to a large mixing bowl. Sprinkle with all-purpose flour, cinnamon, and salt, and stir to combine.

3 Flour a work surface. Roll sheets of puff pastry into two 12-inch (30.5cm) squares. Cut each square into 4 even pieces. Chill pastry squares in the refrigerator for 20 minutes.

4 In a small bowl, beat eggs with water. Brush the edges of each pastry square with egg wash. Place about ⅓ cup apple mixture on one-half of a pastry square. Fold over diagonally and press the edges to close securely. Use a fork to decorate and seal the edges. Repeat with all squares.

5 Place the turnovers on the prepared baking sheets and brush with more egg wash. Make small slits in tops of the turnovers with a sharp knife for steam to escape. Bake for 20 to 23 minutes or until golden brown.

For **Ginger & Pear Turnovers**, replace the apples with pears, leave out the rum, and substitute 2 tablespoons chopped candied ginger for the cranberries.

INFUSION TYPE:
Canna-butter

PREP TIME:
30 minutes

COOK TIME:
30 minutes

SERVING SIZE:
1 turnover

YIELD:
8 turnovers

STORAGE
Keep in an airtight container in the refrigerator for up to 5 days.

Brown Butter Elephant Ears

Ingredients:

3 tablespoons unsalted butter

3 tablespoons canna-butter

2 cups granulated sugar, divided

1 (17.3oz; 490g) package frozen puff pastry, thawed according to package directions

Dietary Notes:
Nut free

Also known as palmiers, elephant ears are perfect for an afternoon snack. A few brushes of brown butter lend these flaky treats a dark caramel richness.

1 Heat the oven to 340°F (170°C). In a medium skillet over medium heat, stir unsalted butter occasionally for 10 to 15 minutes or until toasty brown. Remove from heat and stir in canna-butter. Allow mixture to cool for 15 to 20 minutes.

2 Sprinkle 1 cup sugar onto a large work surface. Unfold each puff pastry sheet and press into sugar. Distribute another ½ cup sugar on top of the sheets. With a rolling pin, roll sheets into 12×12-inch (30.5×30.5cm) squares. Brush sheets with half the melted butter mixture and sprinkle with the remaining ½ cup sugar.

3 Tightly roll two opposite sides of each pastry sheet inward so they meet in the middle, like a rounded heart. Wrap rolled logs in plastic wrap and refrigerate for 30 minutes. Slice each log into 18 slices and place slices cut side up on two baking sheets lined with parchment paper.

4 Brush the remaining half of the melted butter on top. Bake for 30 minutes or until golden. Cool before serving.

INFUSION TYPE:
Canna-butter

PREP TIME:
1 hour

COOK TIME:
45 minutes

SERVING SIZE:
4 elephant ears

YIELD:
36 elephant ears

STORAGE
Keep in an airtight container at room temperature for up to 4 days.

Serve the elephant ears
with a cup of tea or coffee
as a warm, satisfying
complement.

Add some sliced strawberries or bananas to the filling for a twist on the traditional s'mores flavor.

S'mores Hand Pies

Ingredients:

- 1 package (2 crusts) refrigerated unbaked pie crusts
- 2 tablespoons plus 2 teaspoons canna-butter, melted
- 1 cup marshmallow spread
- 4 double graham crackers (such as Honey Maid Fresh Stacks), crumbled
- 1 cup semisweet chocolate chips
- 1 large egg, lightly beaten

Dietary Notes:
None

The melted chocolate, crunchy graham crackers, and gooey marshmallow spread in these small pies bring you all the deliciousness of s'mores—but without the sticky mess.

1 Heat the oven to 340°F (170°C). Line two baking sheets with parchment paper and set aside.

2 Place pie crusts on a floured work surface and roll out slightly using a rolling pin. Using a small, overturned bowl with a 6-inch (15cm) diameter, press into dough to cut out 8 circles. Brush each circle with 1 teaspoon canna-butter.

3 Place 2 tablespoons marshmallow spread on each circle. Equally distribute graham cracker crumbs across half the circles, leaving a ½-inch (1.25cm) rim. Top with semisweet chocolate chips.

4 Using a pastry brush, paint the edges of the circles with egg. Fold over the circles and press to seal. Use a fork to make indentations around the crusts. Use a sharp knife to make vents for steam.

5 Bake for 12 to 14 minutes or until golden brown. Allow to cool a bit before serving.

INFUSION TYPE:
Canna-butter

PREP TIME:
15 minutes

COOK TIME:
14 minutes

SERVING SIZE:
1 hand pie

YIELD:
8 hand pies

STORAGE
Keep in an airtight container at room temperature for up to 3 days.

Rustic Peach & Berry Crostata

Ingredients:

1¾ cups all-purpose flour, divided

6 tablespoons granulated sugar, divided

Pinch salt

4 tablespoons cold canna-butter, diced

11 tablespoons cold unsalted butter, diced, divided

5 tablespoons ice water

4 medium ripe peaches, sliced into wedges

1 cup blueberries

1 cup sliced strawberries

1 tablespoon vanilla extract

Dietary Notes:
None

Whether sweet or savory, crostata is a beautiful, rustic-looking pastry resembling a free-form tart or pie. This dessert's medley of peaches, blueberries, and strawberries is fresh and flavorful.

1 In a medium bowl, combine 1½ cups all-purpose flour, 3 tablespoons sugar, and salt. Add canna-butter and 8 tablespoons unsalted butter, and work into flour mixture until it resembles coarse oatmeal. Add ice water and mix until dough comes together. Wrap in plastic wrap and chill in the refrigerator for 30 minutes.

2 Heat the oven to 340°F (170°C). In a large bowl, combine peaches, blueberries, strawberries, the remaining ¼ cup all-purpose flour, the remaining 3 tablespoons sugar, and vanilla extract.

3 On a floured surface, roll out the dough into a circle ⅛ inch (3mm) thick. Place the fruit mixture on the crust, leaving a 1-inch (2.5cm) border around the edges. Fold the crust up around the edge. Dot the fruit with the remaining 3 tablespoons unsalted butter.

4 Bake for 25 to 30 minutes or until the fruit is bubbling and the crust is golden brown.

INFUSION TYPE:
Canna-butter

PREP TIME:
45 minutes

COOK TIME:
30 minutes

SERVING SIZE:
1 slice

YIELD:
12 slices

STORAGE
Keep loosely covered in plastic wrap on a plate in the refrigerator for up to 5 days.

To avoid trouble removing the crostata from a pan with sides, you can bake it on an inverted pan.

Pistachio & Honey Baklava

Ingredients:

1lb (450g) pistachios

10 tablespoons canna-butter, melted

6 tablespoons unsalted butter, melted

1 (16oz; 450g) package phyllo dough

1 cup water

1 cup granulated sugar

1 teaspoon vanilla extract

½ cup honey

Dietary Notes:

None

TAKE IT HIGHER

For a vegan dessert, use canna-coconut oil instead of canna-butter and agave nectar instead of honey.

The earthy, nutty, sweet flavors of the pistachio and honey pair wonderfully with the cannabis in this flaky treat. And don't be intimidated by the phyllo dough—it's extremely forgiving.

1 Heat the oven to 340°F (170°C). Spray the bottom and the sides of a 9×13-inch (23×33cm) baking pan with nonstick cooking spray. Set aside.

2 In a food processor, chop pistachios into a medium-fine texture. Set aside. Combine melted canna-butter and unsalted butter in a medium bowl. Set aside.

3 Unroll phyllo dough. Cut whole stack in half to fit the pan. Place the stacks on your work surface and cover the dough with a dampened cloth to keep it from drying out as you work. Place 2 sheets of dough in the pan and brush with butter mixture using a pastry brush. Repeat with remaining dough until you have 12 sheets layered. Sprinkle 3 tablespoons chopped pistachios on top.

4 Top chopped pistachios with 2 sheets of phyllo dough and brush with butter mixture. Repeat layering pistachios and dough and brushing with butter mixture until you run out of nuts or phyllo dough. End with 8 sheets layered on top, brushing butter mixture between every 2 sheets of dough.

5 Use a sharp knife to cut the baklava into 30 pieces. Bake for about 50 minutes or until the baklava is golden and crisp.

6 While the baklava is baking, in a small saucepan over medium-high heat, boil water and sugar until sugar is melted. Add vanilla and honey, and simmer slowly over medium heat for about 45 minutes. Remove the baklava from the oven and immediately pour sauce over it. Allow to cool before serving.

INFUSION TYPE:

Canna-butter

PREP TIME:

20 minutes

COOK TIME:

50 minutes

SERVING SIZE:

1 piece

YIELD:

30 pieces

STORAGE

Keep tightly wrapped in plastic wrap in the refrigerator for up to 1 month.

cakes

Tres Leches Cake

Ingredients:

1 cup all-purpose flour

1½ teaspoons baking powder

Pinch salt

5 large eggs, separated

4 tablespoons canna-butter, melted and cooled, divided

1 cup plus 3 tablespoons granulated sugar, divided

4 teaspoons vanilla extract, divided

¼ cup whole milk

1 (12 fl oz; 350ml) can evaporated milk

1 (14 fl oz; 400ml) can condensed milk

2½ cups heavy cream, divided

1 tablespoon unsalted butter, melted and cooled

Dietary Notes:
None

TAKE IT HIGHER
You can also make this as one big cake. Simply butter and flour a 9×13-inch (23×33cm) pan, combine ingredients as directed, and bake for 30 minutes or until the center is set.

These are the moistest little cakes ever. The sweet and creamy flavors are pure and simple in each dreamy, pillowy bite.

1 Heat the oven to 340°F (170°C). Butter and flour one 24-cup muffin tin or two 12-cup muffin tins, filling empty cavities with water, and set aside. In a medium bowl, mix together all-purpose flour, baking powder, and salt. Set aside.

2 Divide egg whites and egg yolks into different medium bowls. In one bowl, beat yolks, 2 tablespoons canna-butter, and ¾ cup sugar with an electric mixer at medium speed until pale yellow. Add 2 teaspoons vanilla extract and whole milk, and beat at low speed until incorporated.

3 In the other bowl, beat egg whites at medium-high speed for 2 minutes or until soft peaks form. Add ¼ cup sugar and continue to beat at medium-high speed until whites are stiff.

4 Combine yolk and flour mixtures. Gently fold in the egg white mixture and then spoon batter into muffin tin or tins. Bake for 20 minutes or until center is set. Remove, poke holes in the tops with a fork, and allow to cool.

5 In a medium bowl, combine evaporated milk, condensed milk, ½ cup heavy cream, the remaining 2 tablespoons canna-butter, and unsalted butter. Pour over the cakes.

6 Beat the remaining 2 cups heavy cream, the remaining 3 tablespoons sugar, and the remaining 2 teaspoons vanilla extract with an electric mixer at medium speed until fluffy. Spread over cooled cakes.

INFUSION TYPE:
Canna-butter

PREP TIME:
20 minutes

COOK TIME:
20 minutes

SERVING SIZE:
1 mini cake

YIELD:
16 mini cakes

STORAGE
Keep in an airtight container in the refrigerator for up to 3 days.

For an attractive presentation, sprinkle additional sliced almonds on top before serving.

Almond & Olive Oil Cake

Ingredients:

1½ cups all-purpose flour

2 teaspoons baking powder

¼ teaspoon salt

1 cup granulated sugar

3 large eggs

1 tablespoon orange zest

1 teaspoon almond extract

¼ cup half-and-half

9 tablespoons extra-virgin olive oil

3 tablespoons canna-coconut oil, melted

¾ cup sliced almonds

2 tablespoons confectioners' sugar

Dietary Notes:
None

Cakes made with olive oil are incredibly moist and textured. For this dessert, the sweet almond flavor tastes perfect with the richness of the oil. You'll savor the cake with each terrific bite.

1 Heat the oven to 340°F (170°C). Line an 8-inch (20cm) cake pan with parchment paper and set aside.

2 In a medium bowl, combine all-purpose flour, baking powder, and salt.

3 In a large bowl, combine sugar, eggs, orange zest, and almond extract. Beat with a mixer on medium speed for 2 to 3 minutes or until light and fluffy.

4 With the mixer running on medium-low speed, add half-and-half followed by extra-virgin olive oil and canna-coconut oil in a stream.

5 Stir in the flour mixture on low speed until just blended. Pour batter into the prepared pan and top with sliced almonds.

6 Bake for 35 to 37 minutes or until a toothpick inserted into the center comes out clean. Remove from the oven and cool on a wire rack. Transfer to a serving dish and dust with confectioners' sugar before serving.

INFUSION TYPE:
Canna-coconut oil

PREP TIME:
20 minutes

COOK TIME:
37 minutes

SERVING SIZE:
1 slice

YIELD:
9 slices

STORAGE
Keep tightly wrapped in plastic wrap at room temperature for up to 5 days.

Ingredients

3½ cups whole milk, divided

1 tablespoon lemon juice

1¾ cups all-purpose flour

3¾ cups granulated sugar, divided

1¼ cups unsweetened cocoa powder, divided

2 teaspoons baking soda

1 teaspoon baking powder

2 large eggs

1 cup cooled brewed coffee

¼ cup vegetable oil

¼ cup canna-coconut oil

½ teaspoon vanilla extract

3 tablespoons cornstarch

Pinch salt

4 tablespoons unsalted butter, divided

1 cup semisweet chocolate chips

Dietary Notes
Nut free

TAKE IT HIGHER

For a flavor variation, add 1 teaspoon espresso powder or 1 teaspoon peppermint extract to the pudding before pouring it over the cake.

Rich chocolate pudding and fudgy frosting turn the classic chocolate pudding cake on its head. The layers of moist cake, creamy pudding, and thick frosting make each bite a joy.

1 Heat the oven to 340°F (170°C). Spray a 9×13-inch (23×33cm) baking pan with nonstick cooking spray and set aside. In a small bowl, mix 1 cup whole milk with lemon juice. Set aside.

2 In a large bowl, combine flour, 1¾ cups sugar, ¾ cup unsweetened cocoa powder, baking soda, and baking powder. Add milk-lemon mixture, eggs, coffee, vegetable oil, canna-coconut oil, and vanilla extract to the flour mixture and stir until well combined. Pour into the prepared pan.

3 Bake for 35 to 40 minutes or until a toothpick inserted into the center comes out clean. Allow to cool while you make the pudding.

4 In a small saucepan over medium heat, combine ¾ cup sugar, the remaining ½ cup unsweetened cocoa powder, cornstarch, and salt, mixing well. Stir in 2¼ cups whole milk. Turn the heat to medium-high and stir constantly until the mixture comes to a boil. Allow to boil for 1 minute, stirring frequently. Remove from heat and stir in 2 tablespoons unsalted butter.

5 Allow the chocolate pudding to cool for 5 minutes, stirring occasionally. Poke cake all over with a knife. Pour warm pudding over slightly warm cake. Lightly tap the pan on the counter to allow the pudding to seep into the cake. Cover and refrigerate for at least 4 hours or overnight.

6 In a small saucepan over medium-high heat, combine the remaining ¼ cup whole milk, the remaining 2 tablespoons unsalted butter, and the remaining 1¼ cups sugar. Boil for 1 minute. Remove from heat and stir in semisweet chocolate chips. Whisk until smooth and shiny. Immediately pour over cooled cake. Refrigerate for 1 hour or until set.

INFUSION TYPE:

Canna-coconut oil

PREP TIME:

5 to 9 hours, 40 minutes

COOK TIME:

55 minutes

SERVING SIZE:

1 square slice

YIELD:

12 square slices

STORAGE

Keep tightly wrapped in plastic wrap in the refrigerator for up to 5 days.

Chocolate Pudding Cake

Banana Cream Roulade

Ingredients:

½ cup confectioners' sugar, divided

¾ cup all-purpose flour

½ teaspoon baking powder

½ teaspoon baking soda

¼ teaspoon salt

4 large eggs, divided

1¼ cups granulated sugar, divided

4 medium bananas, divided

2 cups whole milk

1 tablespoon cornstarch

3 tablespoons canna-butter

½ teaspoon vanilla extract

1¼ cups heavy cream

Dietary Notes:
Nut free

TAKE IT HIGHER
You can top the rolled roulade with extra whipped cream and chopped nuts or coconut for added flair.

The banana sponge cake and creamy custard in this tasty dessert might bring to mind the texture of those little snack cakes you used to eat at school.

1 Heat the oven to 375°F (190°C). Line a 15×10-inch (38×25cm) rimmed baking sheet with parchment paper and set aside. Place a clean kitchen towel on your work surface and sift ¼ cup confectioners' sugar over it evenly. Set aside.

2 In a small bowl, whisk together all-purpose flour, baking powder, baking soda, and salt. In a large bowl, whisk 3 eggs and 1 cup granulated sugar until completely combined. Mash 2 bananas and stir into the egg mixture. Add the flour mixture to the egg mixture and stir to combine. Transfer to the prepared pan and bake for 13 to 15 minutes or until cake springs back at touch.

3 Remove from the oven and carefully flip cake out onto the prepared kitchen towel. Remove the parchment paper from the cake and roll in the towel, starting at one of the shorter sides. Let the cake cool completely in the towel roll.

4 While the cake is cooling, in a double boiler over medium heat, combine the remaining 1 egg, whole milk, the remaining ¼ cup granulated sugar, and cornstarch. Whisk occasionally for 10 to 15 minutes or until mixture thickens and coats the back of a spoon. Remove from heat and stir in canna-butter and vanilla extract. Allow to cool for at least 15 minutes.

5 Use an electric mixer with a whisk attachment to beat heavy cream at medium speed for 7 to 8 minutes or until cream takes on firm peaks. Fold whipped cream into cooled custard and stir until just combined. Unroll cake and remove the towel. Slice the remaining 2 bananas and layer the cake with banana slices. Spread the custard mixture on top.

6 Roll up the roulade in the direction it was rolled with the towel. Cover and place in the refrigerator until ready to serve. Sift the remaining ¼ cup confectioners' sugar over the cake before serving.

INFUSION TYPE:
Canna-butter
PREP TIME:
30 minutes
COOK TIME:
30 minutes
SERVING SIZE:
1 slice
YIELD:
9 slices

STORAGE
Keep tightly wrapped in plastic wrap or in an airtight container in the refrigerator for up to 5 days.

puddings & sauces

Coconut Pot de Crème with Mango Coulis

Ingredients:

4 large egg yolks

½ cup granulated sugar

1 teaspoon vanilla extract

1 (14 fl oz; 400ml) can coconut milk

½ cup heavy cream

4 teaspoons canna-butter

1 cup coconut flakes

1 ripe mango, peeled and chopped

2 teaspoons lime zest

2 teaspoons honey (optional)

Dietary Notes:

Gluten free

With its super-smooth texture, this dessert will make you want to continue eating it forever. The tangy mango sauce is a luxurious and refreshing complement to the coconut flavor.

1 Heat the oven to 325°F (160°C). In a medium heatproof bowl, whisk egg yolks, sugar, and vanilla extract for 20 seconds or until thoroughly combined. In a medium saucepan over medium heat, bring coconut milk, heavy cream, and canna-butter to a gentle simmer. Remove from heat.

2 Whisk ½ cup hot coconut milk mixture into egg mixture. Slowly pour egg–coconut milk mixture into remaining hot coconut milk mixture and whisk until thoroughly combined. Add coconut flakes and stir. Divide pot de crème mixture between four oven-safe 4-ounce (120ml) ramekins.

3 Place the ramekins in a pan partially filled with warm water; the water should come halfway up the ramekins. Bake for 55 minutes or until custard is set in center. Cool on wire racks for 20 minutes. Place in the refrigerator for at least 1 hour. In a blender, purée mango, lime zest, and honey (if using) until smooth. Pour on top of pots de crème before serving.

INFUSION TYPE:
Canna-butter

PREP TIME:
1 hour, 25 minutes

COOK TIME:
1 hour

SERVING SIZE:
1 pot de crème

YIELD:
4 pots de crème

STORAGE
Keep tightly wrapped in plastic wrap in the refrigerator for up to 3 days.

Make frozen pudding pops by pouring the mixture into popsicle molds with sticks and freezing until firm.

Old-Fashioned Butterscotch Pudding

Ingredients:

3 tablespoons cornstarch

2¼ cups whole milk, divided

2 tablespoons unsalted butter

2 tablespoons canna-butter

1 cup loosely packed dark brown sugar

Pinch salt

2 large eggs

1 teaspoon vanilla extract

Dietary Notes:

Gluten free

This quick and easy-to-make pudding combines butter and dark brown sugar into a nostalgic treat. It's just like what Grandma used to make—with one notable exception.

1 In a medium bowl, mix cornstarch and ¼ cup whole milk until smooth. Set aside.

2 In a medium saucepan over medium heat, melt unsalted butter and canna-butter. Mix in dark brown sugar and salt, and remove from heat.

3 Add the remaining 2 cups whole milk to the pan and whisk for 15 seconds to combine. Add cornstarch mixture and whisk for 15 more seconds. Whisk in eggs.

4 Return the pan to the stove. Over medium heat, bring mixture to a gentle simmer, stirring almost constantly, for 8 to 10 minutes or until it starts to thicken. (Pudding will continue to thicken as it cools.)

5 Remove from heat and stir in vanilla extract. Pour into a large bowl and refrigerate for at least 1 hour.

INFUSION TYPE:
Canna-butter

PREP TIME:
1 hour, 15 minutes

COOK TIME:
12 minutes

SERVING SIZE:
½ cup

YIELD:
3 cups

STORAGE
Keep tightly wrapped in plastic wrap in the refrigerator for up to 5 days.

Pink Grapefruit Citrus Curd

Ingredients:
1 cup fresh pink grapefruit juice (about 2 large grapefruit)

3 tablespoons pink grapefruit zest (about 2 large grapefruit)

3 large eggs

3 large egg yolks

¼ cup granulated sugar

2 tablespoons honey

⅛ teaspoon salt

4 tablespoons canna-butter, softened

Dietary Notes:
Gluten free, dairy free

A good curd is a beautiful thing. It has zing. It's tangy and tart while also being sweet and creamy. And it's so easy to enjoy spread on or mixed with your favorite foods.

1 In small saucepan over medium-high heat, bring pink grapefruit juice to a boil. Reduce heat to medium-low and simmer for 5 minutes or until juice is reduced by half. Remove from heat and allow the juice to cool.

2 In a double boiler over medium heat, whisk together reduced pink grapefruit juice, pink grapefruit zest, eggs, egg yolks, sugar, honey, and salt. Cook, whisking constantly, for 5 to 7 minutes or until thickened. Remove from heat and stir in canna-butter 1 tablespoon at a time until combined.

3 Pour into one jar (16 ounces; 470ml) or two jars (8 ounces; 235ml) with lids and let cool for at least 15 minutes.

INFUSION TYPE:
Canna-butter

PREP TIME:
25 minutes

COOK TIME:
15 minutes

SERVING SIZE:
2 tablespoons

YIELD:
1½ cups

Spread the curd on toast or swirl it into your favorite yogurt for a truly decadent breakfast.

STORAGE
Keep in an airtight jar or jars in the refrigerator for up to 1 week.

Serve this sauce on ice cream, pound cake, crêpes, or brownies. Or mix it with milk for chocolate milk.

Hot Fudge Sauce

Ingredients:
5 tablespoons canna-butter

3 tablespoons unsalted butter

¾ cup unsweetened cocoa powder

1 cup heavy cream

¾ cup firmly packed light brown sugar

½ cup granulated sugar

1 teaspoon vanilla extract

Pinch salt

Dietary Notes:
Gluten free

You've probably never had a hot fudge sauce like this. You'll find new ways to use it all the time. It's just so delicious!

1 In a medium saucepan over medium heat, combine canna-butter, unsalted butter, unsweetened cocoa powder, heavy cream, light brown sugar, and granulated sugar. Stir occasionally for about 5 minutes or until butter is melted and ingredients are mixed well.

2 Allow sauce to simmer gently for 3 to 5 minutes, stirring frequently. Remove sauce from heat.

3 Stir in vanilla extract and salt. Serve immediately or allow to cool before storing.

INFUSION TYPE:
Canna-butter

PREP TIME:
5 minutes

COOK TIME:
10 minutes

SERVING SIZE:
2 tablespoons

YIELD:
About 2 cups

STORAGE
Keep in a covered jar in the refrigerator for up to 2 weeks.

Salted Toffee Sauce

Ingredients:

7 tablespoons canna-butter

9 tablespoons unsalted butter

1 cup heavy cream

1 cup firmly packed dark brown sugar

½ teaspoon salt

Dietary Notes:

Gluten free

This sauce strikes just the right balance of sweet and salty. Keep a jar in the fridge and pour over ice cream when any of your cannabis-loving friends stop by.

1 In a medium saucepan over medium-low heat, combine canna-butter, unsalted butter, heavy cream, dark brown sugar, and salt. Bring to a simmer, stirring frequently.

2 Continue to simmer for 10 minutes until sauce begins to reduce in size and thicken. Remove from heat and allow to cool slightly before serving.

INFUSION TYPE:

Canna-butter

PREP TIME:

5 minutes

COOK TIME:

15 minutes

SERVING SIZE:

2 tablespoons

YIELD:

2½ cups

Enjoy this sauce with brownies, ice cream, waffles, apple slices, or coffee. Or simply eat it with a spoon!

STORAGE

Keep in a covered bowl or other airtight container in the refrigerator for up to 2 weeks. If you want, reheat over low heat on the stove before serving.

For a heavenly
breakfast, spread
2 tablespoons on a slice
of toasted brioche bread.

Chocolate & Hazelnut Spread

Ingredients:

1 cup (about 5oz; 140g) skinned hazelnuts

2 tablespoons granulated sugar

1 cup (about 8oz; 225g) semisweet chocolate chips

5 tablespoons plus 1 teaspoon canna-butter

½ cup heavy cream

½ teaspoon salt

Dietary Notes:

Gluten free

Rich chocolate pairs beautifully with earthy hazelnuts in this creamy, dreamy spread. Better than store-bought, this cannabis-infused treat isn't just for breakfast anymore.

1 Preheat the oven to 350° (180°C). Spread hazelnuts on a rimmed baking sheet and toast for 10 to 15 minutes or until nuts begin to brown and become aromatic.

2 In a food processor, purée hazelnuts and sugar for 1 minute or until smooth and creamy.

3 In a double boiler over medium heat, heat semisweet chocolate chips for 5 to 10 minutes or until fully melted. Remove from heat and stir in canna-butter until dissolved.

4 Whisk in heavy cream and salt to fully incorporate. Stir in hazelnut purée.

5 Pour into one jar (16 ounces; 470ml) or two jars (8 ounces; 235ml) with lids.

INFUSION TYPE:
Canna-butter
PREP TIME:
5 minutes
COOK TIME:
25 minutes
SERVING SIZE:
2 tablespoons
YIELD:
2 cups

STORAGE
Keep in the refrigerator for up to 4 weeks or at room temperature for up to 4 days.

chocolates, caramels & candies

White Chocolate Granola Bites

Ingredients:

1½ cups granola

3 tablespoons canna-butter, melted, divided

2 cups white chocolate melts

Dietary Notes:
None

When you coat granola in infused white chocolate, you get something that's greater than the sum of its parts. These indescribably delicious bites will keep you coming back for more—and that's a promise.

1 Heat the oven to 250°F (120°C). On a rimmed baking sheet, mix granola and 2 tablespoons canna-butter. Place the baking sheet in the oven for 5 minutes.

2 Remove the baking sheet and stir until the granola is completely mixed with canna-butter. Return the baking sheet to the oven for 15 minutes, stirring every 5 minutes. Remove from the oven and allow granola to cool completely.

3 In a double boiler over medium heat, combine white chocolate melts and the remaining 1 tablespoon canna-butter. Stir for 5 to 7 minutes or until white chocolate is fully melted and thoroughly combined with canna-butter. Remove from heat.

4 Stir cooled granola into white chocolate mixture. Drop by heaping tablespoons onto parchment paper and allow to cool fully before serving.

INFUSION TYPE:
Canna-butter
PREP TIME:
10 minutes
COOK TIME:
30 minutes
SERVING SIZE:
2 granola bites
YIELD:
32 granola bites

STORAGE
Keep in an airtight container at room temperature for up to 1 week.

White chocolate melts are often
near the chocolate chips at the
store, but white chocolate chips
will also work.

Chocolate-Dipped Dried Mango

Ingredients:

1 cup dark chocolate chips

2 tablespoons canna-coconut oil

12 large pieces unsweetened dried mango

6 tablespoons shredded coconut (optional)

Dietary Notes:

Gluten free, vegan

The concentrated flavor of dried mango makes it a great snack. When it's dipped in dark chocolate and sprinkled with coconut, you have a heart-healthy indulgence.

1 Line a baking sheet with parchment paper and set aside. In a double boiler over medium heat, combine chocolate chips and canna-coconut oil.

2 Stir for 5 to 7 minutes or until chocolate is fully melted and thoroughly combined with canna-coconut oil. Remove from heat.

3 With a fork or your hands, dip each mango piece into the melted chocolate and let any excess drip back into the bowl. Place dipped mango pieces on the prepared baking sheet.

4 Sprinkle shredded coconut (if using) over the dipped mango pieces. Refrigerate for 30 minutes or until chocolate is set.

INFUSION TYPE:

Canna-coconut oil

PREP TIME:

50 minutes

COOK TIME:

7 minutes

SERVING SIZE:

2 mango pieces

YIELD:

12 mango pieces

STORAGE

Keep covered in an airtight container in the refrigerator for up to 6 weeks or in the freezer for up to 6 months.

For an easy variation, substitute chopped pistachios for the shredded coconut in equal amount.

Chocolate Bark with Candied Pecans & Ginger

Ingredients:

2 tablespoons canna-butter

1 cup pecan halves

2 tablespoons firmly packed light or dark brown sugar

2 cups dark chocolate chips

2 tablespoons crystallized ginger

Dietary Notes:

Gluten free

Dark chocolate helps crunchy caramelized pecans and spicy-sweet ginger shine in this treat. If you can stand to give it away, chocolate bark makes an excellent gift.

1 In a small saucepan over low heat, heat canna-butter for 2 to 3 minutes or until fully melted. Add pecan halves and stir for 3 to 5 minutes or until fragrant and nutty. Mix in light brown sugar, stirring constantly, for about 1 minute or until pecans are coated evenly and have begun to caramelize. Remove from heat.

2 Spread caramelized pecans on parchment paper and allow to cool. Roughly chop pecans and set aside.

3 In a double boiler over medium heat, stir dark chocolate chips for 5 to 7 minutes or until completely melted.

4 On a baking sheet lined with parchment paper, spread the melted chocolate. Sprinkle pecans and crystallized ginger evenly on top. Set aside for 1 to 2 hours or until chocolate has set. Cut or break bark into 6 even pieces.

INFUSION TYPE:
Canna-butter

PREP TIME:
1 to 2 hours, 5 minutes

COOK TIME:
15 minutes

SERVING SIZE:
1 piece

YIELD:
6 pieces

STORAGE
Keep covered in an airtight container in the refrigerator for up to 6 weeks or in the freezer for up to 6 months.

This is a great recipe to tweak. Swap the pecans and ginger for your favorite nuts and dried fruit.

Because the powder can be absorbed, re-roll the truffles in the chili powder-cocoa mixture to freshen.

Ancho Chile Truffles

Ingredients:

⅔ cup heavy cream

5 tablespoons canna-butter, divided

3 teaspoons ancho chile powder, divided

2 teaspoons ground cinnamon

Dash salt

½lb (225g) bittersweet chocolate, chopped

1 teaspoon unsweetened cocoa powder

Dietary Notes:

Gluten free

The creaminess of the chocolate ganache and the kick of the ancho chile powder give you a sweet-and-spicy treat that's truly delightful on your tongue.

1 Line a 9×13-inch (23×33cm) baking pan with parchment paper and set aside. In a medium saucepan over medium-low heat, combine heavy cream, 3 tablespoons canna-butter, 2 teaspoons ancho chile powder, cinnamon, and salt. Bring mixture to a boil, cover, and remove from heat. Let stand for 2 hours.

2 Return the saucepan to medium-low heat. Once it reaches a simmer, remove from heat and add bittersweet chocolate and the remaining 2 tablespoons canna-butter. Stir for 2 to 3 minutes or until chocolate is melted and mixture is smooth. Pour into the prepared baking pan and chill in the refrigerator for 4 hours.

3 Using a spoon and your hands, form mixture into sixteen 1-inch (2.5cm) balls. Place balls on a clean baking sheet lined with parchment paper and chill in the refrigerator for 30 minutes.

4 In a small bowl, combine the remaining 1 teaspoon ancho chile powder and cocoa powder. Roll balls in powder and place back on the parchment paper.

INFUSION TYPE:
Canna-butter

PREP TIME:
6 hours,
30 minutes

COOK TIME:
10 minutes

SERVING SIZE:
1 truffle

YIELD:
16 truffles

STORAGE
Keep in an airtight container in the refrigerator for up to 1 week.

Chocolate-Dipped Nougatine

Ingredients:
¾ cup granulated sugar

⅓ cup light corn syrup

¼ cup chopped pistachios

¾ cup sliced almonds

2 tablespoons canna-butter

1 cup dark chocolate chips

Dietary Notes:
Gluten free

Chewy, crunchy, and velvety textures form this confection—a great addition to your canna-candy repertoire. Although it looks like it took hours of labor, nougatine is super easy to make.

1 Line a baking sheet with parchment paper and set aside. In a medium saucepan over medium heat, stir sugar and light corn syrup for 5 to 7 minutes until mixture is melted and starting to caramelize.

2 Mix in pistachios, almonds, and canna-butter, and stir for 2 to 3 minutes to lightly toast almonds. (Don't boil.)

3 Transfer nougatine mixture to the prepared baking sheet and top with an additional sheet of parchment paper. Spread evenly with a rolling pin until about ½ inch (1.25cm) thick. Cut into 12 pieces.

4 In a double boiler over medium heat, melt dark chocolate chips for 5 to 7 minutes.

5 Dip nougatine pieces into melted chocolate, covering just half the nougatine, and return to the parchment-lined baking sheet. Allow chocolate to set for at least 1 hour before serving.

INFUSION TYPE:
Canna-butter

PREP TIME:
1 hour,
10 minutes

COOK TIME:
17 minutes

SERVING SIZE:
2 pieces

YIELD:
12 pieces

STORAGE
Keep in an airtight container for up to 1 week.

This treat is also tasty with walnuts and hazelnuts. Or dip them in white chocolate for added sweetness.

Pretzel Rods with White Chocolate & Toffee Bits

Ingredients:

¼ cup toffee bits

1 cup white chocolate melts

2 tablespoons canna-butter

6 pretzel rods

Dietary Notes:

None

White chocolate is perhaps the perfect partner to cannabis. When you throw in salted pretzels and toffee, forget it! You'll have an edible that looks and tastes unbelievably terrific.

1 Line a baking sheet with parchment paper and set aside. Pour toffee bits onto a shallow plate near the baking sheet.

2 In a double boiler over medium heat, combine white chocolate melts and canna-butter, stirring occasionally, for 5 to 7 minutes or until white chocolate is completely melted.

3 Dip three-fourths of each pretzel rod into the melted white chocolate, allowing any excess chocolate to drip back into the pot.

4 Roll each pretzel rod in toffee bits and place on the prepared baking sheet. Allow to set for at least 30 minutes.

INFUSION TYPE:

Canna-butter

PREP TIME:

40 minutes

COOK TIME:

7 minutes

SERVING SIZE:

1 pretzel rod

YIELD:

6 pretzel rods

Vary the flavors in this dessert with dark chocolate, all kinds of chopped nuts, or decorative candies.

STORAGE

Keep in an airtight container in the refrigerator for up to 1 month.

Ingredients:

8 slices bacon

¼ cup firmly packed light brown sugar

8 tablespoons canna-butter, softened

2 tablespoons unsalted butter, softened

⅓ cup firmly packed dark brown sugar

⅓ cup confectioners' sugar

1½ cups all-purpose flour

½ teaspoon salt

½ cup toffee bits, divided

1 cup dark chocolate chips

⅓ cup chopped almonds

Dietary Notes:

None

Melt-in-your-mouth buttery shortbread and caramelized bacon are over-the-top good in this totally divine confection.

1 Heat the oven to 350°F (180°C). In a medium bowl, toss bacon and light brown sugar, and arrange in a single layer on a baking sheet.

2 Bake for 20 to 25 minutes or until bacon is golden and crispy. Remove from the oven and allow to cool for 15 to 20 minutes. Chop into small pieces.

3 Reduce the oven temperature to 340°F (170°C). Line a 9×13-inch (23×33cm) baking pan with aluminum foil, spray with nonstick cooking spray, and set aside.

4 In a large bowl, mix canna-butter, unsalted butter, dark brown sugar, and confectioners' sugar with an electric mixer at medium speed until light and fluffy. Gradually add all-purpose flour and salt, mixing until just combined. Stir in ¼ cup toffee bits until they're distributed evenly.

5 Press the dough into the prepared pan and bake for 25 minutes or until golden brown. Remove from the oven, sprinkle with dark chocolate chips, and leave for 3 minutes or until chips are softened.

6 Spread chocolate evenly on top and sprinkle with almonds, bacon, and the remaining ¼ cup toffee bits. Allow to cool for 2 hours or until chocolate is set. Cut into sixteen 2-inch (5cm) bars.

INFUSION TYPE:

Canna-butter

PREP TIME:

2 hours, 20 minutes

COOK TIME:

50 minutes

SERVING SIZE:

1 piece

YIELD:

16 pieces

TAKE IT HIGHER

You can find toffee bits next to the chocolate chips in most grocery stores. As for the chocolate chips used in this recipe, feel free to use semisweet or milk chocolate chips instead of dark.

STORAGE

Keep in an airtight container in the refrigerator for up to 1 week.

Candied Bacon Toffee Squares

Buy toasted pecans or toast
your own at 350°F (180°C) for
5 to 10 minutes or until they
begin to brown.

Bourbon, Pecan & Caramel Corn Clusters

Ingredients:

2 tablespoons vegetable oil

⅓ cup popcorn kernels

4 tablespoons canna-butter

4 tablespoons unsalted butter

1½ cups firmly packed light brown sugar

½ cup light corn syrup

2 tablespoons bourbon

½ teaspoon salt

½ teaspoon baking soda

1 cup chopped toasted pecans

Dietary Notes:
Gluten free

We can't decide if it's the satisfying crunch or the rockin' flavor combination of toasted pecans, smoky bourbon, and rich caramel that's our favorite in this recipe. Taste for yourself and decide!

1 In a medium saucepan with a lid over medium heat, heat vegetable oil with 3 popcorn kernels. As soon as a kernel pops, add the remaining kernels and re-cover the saucepan. Cook, shaking the pan frequently, for 3 minutes or until kernels stop popping. Remove from heat and take off the lid.

2 Line a baking sheet with aluminum foil and spray with nonstick cooking spray. In a large saucepan over medium heat, melt canna-butter and unsalted butter. Stirring frequently, add light brown sugar and light corn syrup, and bring to a boil. Attach a candy thermometer to the side of the pan without it touching the bottom. Continue to boil the mixture without stirring for 8 to 10 minutes or until it reaches 300°F (150°C).

3 Remove the saucepan from the heat and stir in bourbon, salt, and baking soda. Quickly add pecans and popcorn, and stir to coat evenly. Immediately transfer mixture to the prepared baking sheet and carefully group into twenty-four ½-cup clusters. Cool for at least 30 minutes before serving.

INFUSION TYPE:
Canna-butter
PREP TIME:
40 minutes
COOK TIME:
15 minutes
SERVING SIZE:
2 clusters
YIELD:
24 clusters

STORAGE
Keep in an airtight container at room temperature for up to 2 weeks.

Pistachio Caramels

Ingredients:

½ cup canna-butter

2 cups firmly packed dark brown sugar,

½ cup dark corn syrup

2 cups heavy cream, divided

¼ teaspoon salt

1 cup chopped roasted pistachios

2 teaspoons vanilla extract

Dietary Notes:

Gluten free

Pistachios seem to be turning up everywhere these days—and for good reason: They add a rich, nutty flavor to cakes and candies. They also supply a slight—and welcome—crunch.

1 Line an 8-inch (20cm) pan with aluminum foil, spray with nonstick cooking spray, and set aside.

2 In a medium saucepan over low heat, melt canna-butter. Add dark brown sugar, dark corn syrup, 1 cup heavy cream, and salt. Bring to a boil, stirring occasionally, for 12 to 15 minutes or until it reaches 225°F (110°C) on a candy thermometer.

3 Slowly add the remaining 1 cup heavy cream. Bring mixture to a boil and cook for 15 minutes more or until it reaches 250°F (120°C). Remove from heat and add pistachios and vanilla extract. Pour into the prepared pan.

4 Cool for at least 3 hours before removing from the foil and cutting into 48 pieces.

5 Cut wax paper into forty-eight 3-inch (7.5cm) squares. Place each caramel in the center of a wax paper square, roll up the paper around the caramel, and twist the ends of the paper.

INFUSION TYPE:

Canna-butter

PREP TIME:

3 hours, 15 minutes

COOK TIME:

35 minutes

SERVING SIZE:

2 pieces

YIELD:

48 pieces

STORAGE

Keep in an airtight container in a cool place for up to 3 weeks.

For a divine gift, top with fleur de sel and more chopped pistachios, and roll in pretty candy wrapping paper.

Use any flavor of gelatin you like. Or make these candies into lollipops with lollipop molds and sticks.

Grape Lozenges

Ingredients:
¾ cup granulated sugar

½ cup light corn syrup

4 tablespoons canna-coconut oil

1 (3oz; 85g) box grape gelatin

Dietary Notes:
Gluten free

Sweet, strong, and satisfying, these lozenges can bring on the effects of THC more quickly than your standard edible. And they're enticing, so keep them away from children.

1 Spray candy molds with nonstick cooking spray and set aside.

2 In a medium saucepan over medium-high heat, combine sugar, light corn syrup, and canna-coconut oil. Bring to a boil and attach a candy thermometer to the side of the pan, making sure to not let it touch the bottom.

3 Stir frequently for 15 to 20 minutes or until mixture reaches 275°F (140°C). Remove from heat and add grape gelatin. Stir well to combine.

4 Drizzle mixture into the candy molds using a spoon or pour in carefully with a spouted cup.

5 Allow the lozenges to cool before removing them from the molds.

INFUSION TYPE:
Canna-coconut oil

PREP TIME:
5 minutes

COOK TIME:
25 minutes

SERVING SIZE:
1 lozenge

YIELD:
12 lozenges

STORAGE
Toss with caster sugar or confectioners' sugar and keep in an airtight container at room temperature for up to 3 weeks.

Caramel Lollipops

Ingredients:

1 cup granulated sugar

2 tablespoons water

¼ cup light corn syrup

1½ teaspoons apple cider vinegar

1 teaspoon salt

1 vanilla bean, split lengthwise

4 tablespoons canna-butter

Dietary Notes:
Gluten free

Lollipops aren't just for kids anymore. The rich, sweet, buttery taste of these grown-up confections is made to be shared—but you might just want to keep them all to yourself.

1 Lightly spray 24 lollipop molds with nonstick cooking spray and set aside. In a medium saucepan over medium-high heat, combine sugar, water, light corn syrup, apple cider vinegar, and salt. Scrape seeds out of the vanilla bean, and stir seeds and bean into mixture. Bring to a boil.

2 Carefully add canna-butter to the boiling mixture and stir until melted. Insert a candy thermometer, attaching it to the side of the pan without letting it touch the bottom. Stir occasionally for 15 to 20 minutes or until caramel reaches 300°F (150°C).

3 Carefully take out vanilla bean and remove the saucepan from the heat. Allow mixture to cool for 5 minutes or until caramel starts to thicken. Working quickly, drizzle caramel into the lollipop molds using a spoon. If caramel becomes too hard, warm over low heat until it becomes workable. Press lollipop sticks into each while still soft.

4 Allow to set for at least 30 minutes or until completely cool. Remove from molds.

INFUSION TYPE:
Canna-butter

PREP TIME:
45 minutes

COOK TIME:
25 minutes

SERVING SIZE:
2 lollipops

YIELD:
24 lollipops

STORAGE
Keep layered between sheets of wax paper in an airtight container at room temperature for up to 2 weeks or in the refrigerator for up to 1 month.

For a decadent finish, you can dip the fully cooled lollipops in milk chocolate and then chopped nuts.

frozen desserts

Lemon & Basil Granita

Ingredients:

3 cups water

1 cup granulated sugar

4 teaspoons canna-coconut oil

2 teaspoons soy lecithin

Pinch salt

1 cup fresh lemon juice (6 lemons)

2 teaspoons grated lemon zest (1 lemon)

2 tablespoons finely chopped basil

Dietary Notes:

Vegan, gluten free, nut free

Like an adult snow cone, granita is a refreshing summertime treat. The lemon really shines through in this dessert, and the basil adds an imaginative complexity.

1 In a medium saucepan over medium heat, combine water, sugar, canna-coconut oil, and soy lecithin. Simmer for 8 to 10 minutes, whisking occasionally.

2 Allow mixture to cool before pouring into a 9×13-inch (23×33cm) baking pan. Place in the refrigerator and chill for 1 hour. Remove from the refrigerator and add lemon juice, lemon zest, and basil. Mix well.

3 Transfer the pan to the freezer and freeze for 30 minutes or until crystals form around the edges of the pan. Stir and return to the freezer. Repeat this process every 30 minutes for 3 to 4 hours. When there are icy, granular crystals throughout, the granita is ready.

For **Lime & Cilantro Granita**, simply substitute lime for the lemon and cilantro for the basil.

INFUSION TYPE:
Canna-coconut oil

PREP TIME:
1 hour, 10 minutes

COOK TIME:
10 minutes

FREEZE TIME:
4 hours

SERVING SIZE:
1 cup

YIELD:
4 cups

STORAGE
Keep in an airtight container in the freezer for up to 1 month.

Ingredients:

1 cup graham cracker crumbs

1 cup plus 2 tablespoons granulated sugar, divided

4 tablespoons canna-butter, melted

2 cups ricotta cheese, drained

8oz (225g) cream cheese

1 tablespoon cornstarch

4 large eggs

2 teaspoons vanilla extract

Pinch salt

⅓ cup fig jam

Dietary Notes:
None

TAKE IT HIGHER

To make your own fig jam, combine 8 ounces (227g) fresh or dried figs, ½ cup granulated sugar, 2 tablespoons lemon juice, and 2 tablespoons water in a large saucepan. Bring to a simmer over medium heat and cook for 20 minutes or until desired consistency is reached.

Soft and uniquely flavorful, the ricotta in this batter makes for a lighter cheesecake. Plus, the graham cracker crust and fig jam complement each other beautifully.

1 Heat the oven to 340°F (170°C). Wrap the inside of a 9-inch (23cm) springform pan with aluminum foil. Spray with nonstick cooking spray and set aside.

2 In a small bowl, combine graham cracker crumbs, 2 tablespoons sugar, and canna-butter. Press into the bottom of the prepared pan. Chill for 30 minutes in the refrigerator.

3 In a large mixing bowl, add ricotta cheese, cream cheese, the remaining 1 cup sugar, and cornstarch. Mix well with an electric mixer at medium speed. Add eggs one at a time, beating at low speed after each addition. Add vanilla extract and salt, and beat at low speed until incorporated.

4 Remove the crust from the refrigerator. Pour the batter into the crust. Gently swirl fig jam into cheesecake for a marbled effect. Place the pan in a larger pan of hot water so the springform pan is half submerged.

5 Bake for 55 minutes to 1 hour. Cake should be set but still have a slight jiggle. Remove from the larger pan of water and cool on a wire rack until it reaches room temperature.

6 Slide a butter knife around the inside edge of the pan to separate the cheesecake from the pan and then unclamp the outside part of the pan. Chill for 1 hour and then freeze for 4 hours. Allow to sit at room temperature for 10 to 15 minutes before slicing and serving.

INFUSION TYPE:
Canna-butter

PREP TIME:
1 hour, 45 minutes

COOK TIME:
1 hour

FREEZE TIME:
4 hours

SERVING SIZE:
1 slice

YIELD:
12 slices

STORAGE
Keep wrapped tightly in plastic wrap in the freezer for up to 1 month.

Frozen Fig Cheesecake

Roasted Sweet Corn Popsicles

Ingredients:
3 tablespoons canna-coconut oil

3½ cups sweet corn kernels, divided

1 (14oz; 400ml) can condensed milk

4oz (120ml) coconut milk

1 teaspoon vanilla extract

½ teaspoon ground cinnamon

Pinch salt

Dietary Notes:
Gluten free

If you're like many people, you might be skeptical that sweet corn can function as a frozen treat. If you're like us, however, one bite will have you sold.

1 In a medium skillet over medium-high heat, heat canna-coconut oil. Add 3 cups sweet corn kernels and sauté for 5 to 6 minutes or until kernels begin to char. Remove from heat and allow to cool.

2 In a blender, process charred corn kernels, condensed milk, coconut milk, vanilla extract, cinnamon, and salt on low speed for 3 to 4 minutes or until smooth.

3 Stir in the remaining ½ cup sweet corn kernels. Pour the mixture into popsicle molds and freeze for a minimum of 4 hours.

INFUSION TYPE:
Canna-coconut oil

PREP TIME:
10 minutes

COOK TIME:
10 minutes

FREEZE TIME:
4 hours

SERVING SIZE:
1 popsicle

YIELD:
9 popsicles

Spice up the flavor of these pops by adding ½ teaspoon of chili powder and a pinch of cayenne pepper.

STORAGE
Keep in the molds in the freezer for up to 6 months.

No-Churn Vanilla Ice Cream

Ingredients:

1 (14 fl oz; 400ml) can sweetened condensed milk

2 tablespoons canna-butter, softened

1 tablespoon vanilla extract

2 cups heavy cream

Dietary Notes:

Gluten free

Simple and fast to make, this ice cream can be flavored any way you'd like it to be. And the best part is, you don't even need an ice cream maker for it!

1 In a medium bowl, combine sweetened condensed milk, canna-butter, and vanilla extract. In a large bowl, beat heavy cream with a mixer on high for 3 minutes until stiff peaks form.

2 Gently fold the whipped cream into the condensed milk mixture. Pour into a loaf pan and freeze for 8 hours or until firm.

For **Orange & Cardamom Ice Cream**, add the zest of 1 orange, 1 teaspoon ground cardamom, ⅛ teaspoon ground clove, and ¼ teaspoon cinnamon to the condensed milk mixture.

For **Chocolate & Cherry Ice Cream**, add ⅓ cup chopped dark or semisweet chocolate, ⅓ cup cherry jam or preserves, and ½ teaspoon almond extract to the condensed milk mixture.

For **Mint & Chocolate Chip Ice Cream**, add ½ teaspoon mint extract to the condensed milk mixture. After folding in the whipped cream, gently stir in 1 cup finely chopped mint chocolate.

INFUSION TYPE:
Canna-butter

PREP TIME:
10 minutes

COOK TIME:
None

FREEZE TIME:
8 hours

SERVING SIZE:
1 cup

YIELD:
6 cups

STORAGE
Keep in an airtight container in the freezer for up to 2 weeks.

Plum & Wine Granita

Ingredients:
½ cup red wine of choice

1 teaspoon vanilla extract

½ cup granulated sugar

2 tablespoons canna-coconut oil

2lb (1kg) plums, pitted

2 tablespoons honey

Dietary Notes:
Dairy free, gluten free

Granita is a super-easy way to make a frozen treat. If you don't like mixing alcohol and cannabis, don't worry! The alcohol cooks away, leaving only a delicious plum flavor.

1 In a medium saucepan over medium-high heat, combine red wine, vanilla extract, and sugar. Once mixture reaches a boil, reduce heat to medium and simmer for 7 to 10 minutes. Remove from heat and stir in canna-coconut oil. Allow to cool.

2 Blend plums, honey, and cooled wine mixture in a blender at medium speed for 2 to 3 minutes or until smooth. Chill mixture in the refrigerator for 4 hours or up to 1 week.

3 Remove from the refrigerator and blend mixture for 30 seconds to recombine. Pour into a 9×13-inch (23×33cm) baking pan and then freeze.

4 Stir with a fork every 30 minutes for about 4 hours or until a granular texture is achieved.

5 Transfer to an airtight container and return to the freezer if not serving right away. Remove from the freezer 15 minutes before serving.

For **Plum & Wine Sorbet**, pour the mixture into an ice cream maker and follow the manufacturer's directions.

INFUSION TYPE:
Canna-coconut oil

PREP TIME:
4 hours, 40 minutes

COOK TIME:
10 minutes

FREEZE TIME:
4 hours

SERVING SIZE:
½ cup

YIELD:
3 cups

STORAGE
Keep in an airtight container in the freezer for up to 2 weeks.

Glossary

bake   To cook in a dry oven. Dry-heat cooking often results in a crisping of the exterior of the food being cooked. Moist-heat cooking—through methods such as steaming, poaching, and so on—brings a much different, moist quality to the food.

beat   To quickly mix substances.

blend   To completely mix something, usually with a blender or food processor, slower than beating.

boil   To heat a liquid to the point where water is forced to turn into steam, causing the liquid to bubble. To boil something is to insert it into boiling water. A rapid boil is when a lot of bubbles form on the surface of the liquid.

brown   To cook in a skillet, turning, until the food's surface is seared and brown in color, to lock in the juices.

cannabinoids   Chemical compounds in the cannabis plant resin that activate receptors throughout the human body and brain.

cannabis   The scientific name for the marijuana plant.

caramelize   To cook sugar over low heat until it develops a sweet caramel flavor, or to cook vegetables (especially onions) or meat in butter or oil over low heat until they soften, sweeten, and develop a caramel color.

CBD   Cannabidiol, a cannabinoid in cannabis with lots of health benefits. It doesn't have the psychoactive effects of THC.

chop   To cut into pieces, usually qualified by an adverb such as "coarsely chopped" or by a size measurement such as "chopped into ½-inch pieces." "Finely chopped" is much closer to mince.

crystallized ginger   Chopped ginger that has been dried and candied.

custard   A cooked mixture of eggs and milk that's popular as a base for desserts.

dash   A few drops, usually of a liquid, released by a quick shake.

decarboxylate   To convert THCA into THC by heating cannabis.

dice   To cut into small cubes about ¼-inch (.5cm) square.

double boiler   A set of two pots designed to nest together, one inside the other, and provide consistent, moist heat for foods that need delicate treatment. The bottom pot holds water (not quite touching the bottom of the top pot); the top pot holds the food you want to heat.

drizzle   To lightly sprinkle drops of a liquid over food, often as the finishing touch to a dish.

extract   A concentrated flavoring derived from foods or plants through evaporation or distillation. It imparts a powerful flavor without altering the volume or texture of a dish.

fold   To combine a dense mixture and a light mixture with a circular action from the middle of the bowl.

Greek yogurt   A strained yogurt that's a good natural source of protein, calcium, and probiotics. Greek yogurt averages 40 percent more protein per ounce than traditional yogurt.

infusion   A liquid in which flavorful ingredients such as herbs have been soaked or steeped to extract their flavor into the liquid.

Key lime   A very small lime grown primarily in Florida known for its tart taste.

knead   To work dough to make it pliable so it holds gas bubbles as it bakes. Kneading is fundamental in the process of making yeast breads.

marijuana   Slang for the cannabis plant.

pinch   An unscientific measurement for the amount of an ingredient—typically, a dry, granular substance such as an herb or seasoning that you can hold between your finger and thumb.

preheat   To turn on an oven, broiler, or other cooking appliance in advance of cooking so the temperature will be at the desired level when the assembled dish is ready for cooking.

purée   To reduce a food to a thick, creamy texture, typically using a blender or food processor.

reduce   To boil or simmer a broth or sauce to remove some of the water content, resulting in more concentrated flavor and color.

resin   The sticky, oily substance excreted from the cannabis plant containing cannabinoids and terpenes.

sauté   To pan-cook over lower heat than what's used for frying.

simmer   To boil a liquid gently so it barely bubbles.

skillet (also frying pan)   A generally heavy, flat-bottomed, metal pan with a handle designed to cook food over heat on a stovetop or campfire.

skim   To remove fat or other material from the top of liquid.

steam   To suspend a food over boiling water and allow the heat of the steam (water vapor) to cook the food. This quick-cooking method preserves a food's flavor and texture.

terpenes   Aromatic, flavorful oils excreted in the cannabis plant resin.

THC   Tetrahydrocannabinol, the primary cannabinoid found in marijuana. It's psychoactive and responsible for the "high" associated with cannabis.

whisk   To rapidly mix, introducing air into a mixture.

zest   Small slivers of peel, usually from a citrus fruit, such as a lemon, lime, or orange.

Index

About the Authors

Laurie + MaryJane
Laurie + MaryJane is an award-winning marijuana edibles company dedicated to producing high-quality products for the cannabis community since 2014.

Laurie Wolf
Laurie is a graduate of the Culinary Institute of America and has been a food stylist, food editor, recipe developer, and cookbook author for over 30 years. She is a regular contributor and edible recipe developer for *The Cannabist, High Times, Oregon Leaf,* and *Cannabis Now.* A leading voice in marijuana edibles, Laurie's passion for cannabis as a treatment stems from her exposure to her father's end-of-life care, as well as her own successful management of a seizure disorder.

Mary Thigpen
Mary left a career in marketing at a New York investment firm and moved to Portland, Oregon, where she joined her mother-in-law's marijuana edible start-up. A lifelong lover of baking, Mary adores working with her mother-in-law in the kitchen and on writing books.